Contents

Chapter One

It was a gloomy Sunday for the Nair family. The father of Mrs. Nair had passed only a week ago, and everyone was still trying to cope with his absence. Even though all were saddened by his sudden demise, it was young Narendra, who seemed the most affected.

Listening to one of grandfather's stories was one of his favorite pastimes. Every evening, after coming back from school, he would move the small wooden chair closer to the armchair near the window, where his grandfather usually sat reading some book. Sitting down on the small chair and placing his elbows on the armrest, he would spend hours lost in the adventurous tales of ancient kings and queens.

As the family sat down for breakfast, Narendra cast a painful glance at the armchair in the hall. Tears welled in his eyes, and he ran away from the table to his room.

Hurriedly putting down the bowl she was serving from, Mrs. Nair ran after him. Gently knocking on the door, she opened it. Narendra was sitting on the floor beside the bed, his face hidden behind his folded knees.

"Please eat something," said Mrs. Nair.

"Leave me alone," said Narendra.

"You know I can't do that," said his mother, sitting down besides him. Wrapping her hands around his shoulder, she added, "Talk to me! It will help!"

"What is there to talk?" said Narendra. "Grandpa's gone! Just like that! Now there's nothing we can do!"

"We all have to go at some point of time," said Mrs. Nair. "It is inevitable!"

"Why?"

"That is just the way it is!"

Wiping the tears on his sleeve, Narendra asked, "What happens when we die?"

"It's complicated," said Mrs. Nair.

"Tell me, I want to know!"

After a brief moment of silence, Mrs. Nair said, "You remind me of Nachiketas!"

"Who is Nachiketas?" asked Narendra.

"Nachiketas was the boy who had willingly gone to the abode of the

God of Death and asked him the same question that you just did!”
    “Please tell me that story!”
    “Ok,” said Mrs. Nair. “Listen carefully!”

Chapter Two

Thousands of years ago, in a small village in India, there was a priest named Vajashravasa. He was a very wise man and had mastered all the sacred texts of the time.

One day, having become disinterested in the activities of the world, he decided to conduct a sacred ritual known as Vishvajith. This was no ordinary ritual. A person who decided to undertake this ritual was required to give away everything he considered his own in charity, thereby getting freed from all worldly attachments and becoming fit for treading through the spiritual path.

Vajashravasa was not a very rich man. His sole possessions were cows. He had arranged them in a special hall in order to be gifted to anyone who needed it. The ritual had neared completion, when his young son, Nachiketas, arrived at the hall.

The young fellow looked around and noticed that the best of the cows had already been given, and that which remained where of no use to anyone. Nachiketas was a wise boy, and he knew very well that only useful objects were to be given away during such a ritual. Therefore, he began to wonder if there was anything left in his father's possession, which was still fit to be gifted.

Upon contemplation, he realized that he was the last of his father's possession, which was worthy of being given away. Therefore, approaching his father, he asked, "To whom do you give me?"

Even though Vajashravasa realized the reason for his son's query, he did not give an immediate reply, as he wanted to test the willingness of the boy. If Nachiketas's offer to be given away in charity was not sincere, then he would quietly walk away on being neglected.

However, Nachiketas was determined and asked again for a second time, and then, for a third time. Pleased with his son's determination, Vajashravasa said, "I give you to Lord Yama, the God of Death!"

Chapter Three

"Wow," said Narendra. "He is such a cold-hearted father!"

Shaking her head, Mrs. Nair said, "No, dear child, Vajashravasa was not a cold-hearted father. He was a kind-hearted man, and had nothing but love for his son. His reply was not a sudden outburst at being interrupted during the ritual. Instead, it was the result of deep contemplation."

"Why would anyone give their own son to Lord Yama?" asked Narendra.

"He knew from the very beginning that for the successful completion of this ritual, he would have to give everything away, including his only son," said Mrs. Nair. "However, he felt it to be unjust to force such a decision on his son. Therefore, he had decided to wait patiently and see if the years of learning had made his son detached enough to come forward to be willingly given as a gift.

"Now, Vajashravasa did not want to give his son away to anyone who would ask. He wanted this act of his to help his son attain greater wisdom. Therefore, after due thought, he had decided that the best person to gift his son was Lord Yama Himself."

"Why?" asked Narendra.

"The ultimate destination of all those who have been born in this world is death. Whether we like it or not, eventually we will all die. Therefore, Lord Yama, the God of Death, was the true owner of all mortals. Based on the qualities of our actions in the past birth, Lord Yama loans us a suitable body for this birth. When the stipulated period ends, He repossesses that which is rightfully His."

"I see," said Narendra. "What did Nachiketas do when he heard his father's reply?"

Chapter Four

When young Nachiketas heard his father's reply, he saluted him wholeheartedly and set off to the abode of Yama.

After a difficult journey through the Himalayan valleys, Nachiketas finally arrived at the abode of Lord Yama, which was located at the south of Mount Meru. However, he found out from the guards that Lord Yama had gone out.

When he announced the purpose of his visit, the guards were surprised and tried to persuade him to go back because without the permission of their master, they could not grant him access to the sacred abode, and chances were that Lord Yama would return only after a few days.

Determined to fulfill the wishes of his father, the young boy decided to wait until the arrival of Yama. Sitting down besides the golden gate, Nachiketas started to contemplate on the purpose of his father's decision to give him to Lord Yama.

Soon, it occurred to him that he was the first amongst many to visit the abode of Lord Yama, and therefore, he must act as a representative of all those people. That is, he felt that he had a responsibility towards all those mortals, who were going to reluctantly visit Lord Yama at some point of time in the future.

"All mortals fear death because they are not certain as to what will happen to them after death," he thought. "'Will I exist even after death, or will I cease to be?' This is the question that haunts them! This is the question that haunts me too! Right now, I am alive! But soon, I will die! Then what? Is it the end of me? Or is it just a doorway to another realm? Do I have an existence beyond the body?"

Possessed by these questions, Nachiketas decided to find a definite answer from Lord Yama Himself, so that he, as well as all other mortals, can be absolved from the fear of death. Thus, he eagerly awaited the arrival of the God of Death.

Three days and nights passed. Despite repeated attempts from the guards to dissuade him, Nachiketas did not go back. He remained calm and quiet, determined to fulfill the wish of his father.

At the dawn of the fourth day, Lord Yama returned from his journey. He paused as he saw the young boy seated besides the gate and cast an enquiring glance at the guards.

"This boy says his father has gifted him to You, my Lord," said one of the guards. "He has been waiting here to meet You for three days and nights, without either food or water!"

"What?" exclaimed Lord Yama. "Bring some water immediately! A host who does not attend to his guest is doomed forever! No matter what be the purpose of the visit, a host should first quench the thirst of his guest, then satisfy his hunger, offer him a place to rest, and only then enquire about his intention! Therefore, make immediate arrangements for our dear guest! Let him be appeased!"

Lord Yama escorted Nachiketas inside, offered him a comfortable seat, gave him delicious food and water, and then led him to a spacious balcony facing Mount Meru. Offering him a well-cushioned, golden chair, Yama sat besides him.

"Tell me," said Lord Yama, "who are you?"

"I am Nachiketas, son of Vajashravasa!"

"Seldom do mortals travel of their own accord to this place," said Yama. "Even when summoned by me, they are reluctant! Yet, here you are! Calm and content, as if you have reached heaven! Tell me, dear boy, why are you here?"

With a smile, Nachiketas explained, "My father had conducted the ritual known as Vishvajith! In order to complete his undertaking, he has given me as an offering to You!"

Lord Yama rubbed his chin and watched his young guest curiously. After some moments of contemplative silence, he said, "O wise Nachiketas, since you have waited at my doorstep for three days and nights, I promise to fulfill three boons of your choice! Please tell me what you need!"

Contemplating on the offer for some time, Nachiketas said, "Let my kind father be freed from grief about me and attain complete contentment, O Lord Yama, so that he will accept and recognize me, when you relieve me! This is my first wish amongst the three!"

"So be it," said Yama, unable to resist a smile.

Chapter Five

"Why would Nachiketas ask for such a boon?"

"Because he was intelligent," said Mrs. Nair.

"Intelligent? How?"

Smiling at her son, Mrs. Nair explained, "The acute intelligence of Nachiketas is commendable here because by asking a single boon, he has obtained multiple benefits from Yama."

"What benefits?" asked Narendra.

"Vajashravasa was giving away all of his belongings in the ritual so that he could attain that supreme state of existence, wherein he is content with his own self. Therefore, by asking for his father's contentment, Nachiketas has ensured the success of the ritual."

"Ok," said Narendra. "What other benefits did he get?"

"By asking this boon," said Mrs. Nair, "he has also ensured that Lord Yama will send him back."

"Wow," said Narendra.

"However," Mrs. Nair continued, "he realizes that even if he goes back, his father might be reluctant to accept him, because he had been given as an offering to Lord Yama. Therefore, Nachiketas makes sure that his father will receive him without any reluctance whatsoever.

"Thus, through a single boon, Nachiketas has ensured three things."

"Impressive," said Narendra. "He is a genius!"

Mrs. Nair nodded her head in agreement before continuing the story.

*

Glad that his first wish had been granted immediately, Nachiketas said, "In heaven, there is absolutely no fear, for You are not there; nor is there any fear of decay! Having transcended both hunger and thirst, and without any sorrow, they rejoice in heaven! O Yama, I implore You to explain to me, who am full of faith, that sacred ritual, through the performance of which one can attain immortal heaven! This is the second boon that I ask!"

Nodding his head, Lord Yama said, "At a special altar, using a special firewood, a special oblation must be offered to a secret Fire, which is always situated in the heart! Any person who performs this ritual for three times will reach that immortal heaven, where both birth and death are transcended!"

After a brief pause, Yama added, "Since you are the first to ask me about this Fire, I will name it after you! From now on, people will refer to it as the Nachiketas Fire!"

Chapter Six

"What is this ritual that Lord Yama is referring to?" asked Narendra, scratching his head.

Mrs. Nair said, "Even though Lord Yama does not elaborate on the secret of this ritual, He provides us with enough hints to reach the truth on our own."

"I do not comprehend!" said Narendra.

"Lord Yama described that the secret Fire was situated in the heart," said Mrs. Nair. "The term 'heart' is used herein to mean the core of an individual, and not the physical organ that pumps blood. That is, this secret Fire is the ultimate essence of an individual."

"Why is it called a fire?"

"It is called a Fire because It illumines everything for the individual."

"Please elaborate," said Narendra.

"The senses, the mind, and the intellect perform their respective functions due to Its presence. If It did not exist, we will not be able to perceive anything. Therefore, it is the Soul, which is symbolized here as a secret Fire."

"I know that eyes, ears, nose, tongue, and skin are the five senses," said Narendra. "However, I don't know the difference between the mind and the intellect!"

"Mind is a stream of thoughts, while the intellect is the controller of those thoughts," said Mrs. Nair.

"I do not understand!"

"Let me give you an example," said Mrs. Nair. "You know that eating a lot of oily food is not good for your health. You also know that such a food is tasty. Are you following me?"

"Yes!"

"Now, imagine that you have been presented with a heap of fries!"

"Ok!"

"Two thoughts spring in your mind – it is not healthy and it is tasty!"

"Yes," said Narendra.

"At this point, there is an intelligent principle behind the mind, which evaluates both the thoughts and sanctions the right course of action. This is the intellect!"

"I see!"

"If the intellect is dull, then the mind would do as it pleases," said Mrs. Nair. "However, if the intellect is strong, then it forces the mind to do the right thing!"

"I see," said Narendra.

"Do you know the Gayatri Mantra?"

"Yes!"

"Chant it," said Mrs. Nair. "Let me hear!"

Narendra started chanting, *"Om bhoor bhuvah svah, thath savithur varenyam, bhargo devasya dheemahi, dheeyo yo nah prachodayaath!"*

"Good," said his mother. "Now, do you know its meaning?"

"No, I don't," said Narendra.

"It means, 'I meditate on that Lord, who illumines all the three worlds; please inspire my intellect!'"

"Is this mantra meant for the sun?" asked Narendra.

"If you take the three worlds to mean earth, atmosphere, and space, then it is dedicated to the Sun," said Mrs. Nair.

"Does the 'three worlds' have any other meaning?"

"Yes," said Mrs. Nair. "The three worlds represent the senses, the mind and the intellect!"

"Wow," said Narendra. "In that case, the mantra is an invocation to the Soul!"

"Yes," said Mrs. Nair. "Without the Soul, these three can't function. They become inert. Therefore, the Gayatri Mantra invokes the Soul to enliven these three, while making a special request to brighten the intellect, so that we are able to always make the right choice!"

"Maybe I should start chanting this mantra more often," said Narendra.

"Yes, you should," said Mrs. Nair.

"Now," said Narendra. "Please tell me more about the ritual mentioned by Lord Yama!"

"Just as fire, which is ever existent in the wood, manifests itself during friction, the Soul, which is ever existent in the individual, manifests Itself when the individual meditates," said Mrs. Nair. "This process of meditation is the special ritual indicated by Lord Yama."

"What has firewood and oblation got to do with meditation?" asked Narendra.

"The ritual is symbolic, dear child," said Mrs. Nair, "In this ritual, the body is the altar, the intellect is the firewood, the mind is the oblation, and the Soul is the Fire."

"I see," said Narendra, impressed by the symbolism. "That is, we have to steady our body and dissolve our mind in the intellect, thereby realizing the Soul! Is that right?"

"Yes," said Mrs. Nair, smiling. "Now, it is interesting to notice Lord Yama declare that if a person were to perform this ritual for three times, he will transcend both birth and death."

"Yes, I was wondering about it," said Narendra. "Why did he say that?"

"Three times is suggested here because the mind, which is described as the oblation in this symbolic ritual, has three layers – Waking state (conscious mind), dream state (subconscious mind), and deep sleep state (unconscious mind). When these three layers are transcended, the individual attains the Soul, which is a state of supreme peace. This peace is described by Lord Yama as heaven."

Chapter Seven

"This is all very good to hear," said Narendra, "but how is this transcendence really achieved? What should we do to meditate successfully? Please tell me about this!"

"There are many ways in which one can meditate and achieve this transcendence," said Mrs. Nair. "However, I will give you an easy method, which if you follow sincerely, you will certainly succeed!"

"What is it?" asked Narendra.

"First, you must sit in a comfortable position!"

"Should I sit down with folded legs, or should I use a chair?"

"Any position that is comfortable to you is fine," said Mrs. Nair. "The only important thing is that your spine is kept erect!"

"Why?" asked Narendra.

"Because an erect spine keeps you alert!"

"I see!"

"Now," Mrs. Nair said, "close your eyes and place your left palm on your left thigh, while closing your right nostril with your right thumb. Take a slow, deep breath through your left nostril and then close it with your right middle finger. Release you right thumb, and exhale gently through your right nostril. Then, breathe in through your right nostril, close it with the right thumb, and then exhale through the left nostril! Repeat this process for twelve times."

"How do I know that my breathing is gentle enough?"

"When there is no audible sound during breathing, you are doing it right. Remember, the purpose is to relax. Therefore, do not exhaust yourself by breathing violently!"

"Ok," said Narendra. "Is there any way to synchronize my inhalation and exhalation?"

"Yes," said Mrs. Nair. "To achieve this, you could mentally chant the Gayatri Mantra!"

"How?"

"Chant '*om bhoor bhuvah svah*' while inhaling through your left nostril. Then keep your breath till you chant '*thath savitur varenyam*'. Release the breath through your right nostril while chanting '*bhargo devasya dheemahi*'. Then keep the breath out till you chant '*dheeyo yo nah prachodayaath*'. Repeat this process for twelve times!"

"That sounds good," said Narendra. "Is it necessary to chant the mantra?"

"No," said Mrs. Nair. "The mantra is just to guide you to regulate your breathing. Chanting it is not compulsory. In fact, it is better to breathe in silence without any distraction. The only thing that you need to remember is to keep your palm above the nose so that it does not obstruct the flow of air."

"Ok," said Narendra.

"Once you complete this process," said Mrs. Nair, "sit in silence for as long as you can. This breathing process would have calmed you so good that you will be able to meditate peacefully for some time! Practice this early in the morning, if possible! If not, choose any convenient time! Just make sure to do it regularly!"

"Ok!"

"Shall we now proceed to the story of Nachiketas?" asked Mrs. Nair.

"Yes, please," said Narendra.

Chapter Eight

After contemplating on the subtle words of Lord Yama for some time, and having successfully deduced their meaning, Nachiketas said, "There is this doubt regarding the departed; some say that they exist, some say that they don't! I implore you to impart this knowledge to me, for I ask this as the third boon!"

Even though Lord Yama had taught him about the secret of experiencing the Soul situated in the heart through the process of meditation, Nachiketas is not satisfied enough to immediately start practicing it. He is intelligent enough to understand that meditation is not an easy process, and will take great amount of perseverance and dedication to succeed.

*

"How long will it take to realize the Soul?" asked Narendra.

"Well," said Mrs. Nair. "It all depends on the spiritual maturity of the seeker. King Khatvanga attained it in less than an hour, while King Pareekshith took seven days to realize it, and King Bharata had to take two more births to realize it!"

"Wow," said Narendra. "Please tell me the stories of all the three kings in detail!"

"Ok," said Mrs. Nair. "First, I will tell you the story of King Khatvanga!"

Chapter Nine

King Khatvanga was a valiant warrior and was respected even by the celestials. Once, when the demons had launched a full-blown attack on heaven, the celestials approached Khatvanga for help.

Without any delay, Khatvanga accompanied the celestials to heaven and fought a great battle with the demons, which lasted for a very long time.

Despite the best of their attempts, the demons were unable to defeat Khatvanga, and finally ran away from the battlefield, scared for their lives.

Pleased with the prowess of the king, Lord Indra, the king of the celestials, offered him any boon of his choice. Being a wise man, instead of choosing trivial material pleasures, Khatvanga said, "Please tell me how much time I have left in this world!"

After consulting with Lord Yama, the God of Death, Indra said, "I am so sorry, O King, for you have less than an hour to live!"

"Is that so?" asked Khatvanga.

Abandoning his weapons and armor, the king went to a secluded place, sat down with folded legs, closed his eyes, and started meditating.

His focus was so intent that within no time he realized the Soul. As the time for departure arrived, he renounced the body with a content smile on his face.

*

"Wow," said Narendra. "Is that really possible?"

"Yes, dear child," said Mrs. Nair. "It is very much possible for a determined person!"

"Ok," said Narendra. "Now, tell me the story of King Pareekshith!"

Chapter Ten

Pareekshith was a just king, who had always treated his people with respect and love. However, reminding us all that even a moment's lapse of judgment can turn our life upside down, the king once committed a grave mistake, which eventually led to his death.

He was out on a hunting expedition in the forest, when he lost his way and got separated from his troop. Searching for the track that led back home, he came across a hermitage, where a sage was absorbed in deep meditation.

Pareekshith was exhausted and thirsty. Therefore, he approached the sage and asked for some water to drink.

Despite being intelligent enough to know that the sage could not hear him, as he had withdrawn his senses, the king, blinded by exhaustion, was unable to think straight. He felt insulted at the lack of response.

Noticing a dead snake lying nearby, he picked it up and placed it around the neck of the sage. Muttering under his breath, the king then left the hermitage.

Meanwhile, the son of that sage returned from his play. Seeing the dead snake around his father's neck, the boy became furious.

"Whoever did this to my father will die by the bite of a snake at the end of the seventh day," cursed the young boy.

When several hours later, the sage woke from his meditation, his son informed him about all that happened. Through his inner eye, the sage realized that it was King Pareekshith who had put the snake on him.

"It does not befit you to curse other people, my son," said the sage.

"I am sorry, father," said the son. "I got carried away!"

"You must immediately inform our king about the impending doom," said the sage.

Accepting the command of his father, the young boy went to the palace and informed the king of the curse.

Pareekshith, who was already feeling guilty at his actions, renounced the kingdom and went to the shore of River Ganga to meditate. At this time, due to his good fortune, Sage Shuka, the famed son of Sage Vyasa, arrived there.

Enquired by the king, Sage Shuka narrated a series of stories, full of wisdom, known as Srimad Bhaagavata. For seven days, the king sat listening to those stories, all the while contemplating on their hidden meaning.

By the time the snake arrived to kill him, he had realized the Soul and had become fearless. Saluting the snake, he willfully let it bite him, thereby abandoning his body.

*

"Anger is such a curse," said Narendra. "Well, at least the king succeeded in realizing the Soul!"

"Yes," said Mrs. Nair. "Now I will tell you the story of King Bharata!"

"Ok," said Narendra.

Chapter Eleven

Bharata was such a great king that this entire stretch of land, which is popularly known as India, is also called Bhaarata as a tribute to him. He was a just king and always gave first preference for the welfare of his people.

Having ruled the kingdom for a long time, he grew weary of the world and distributed his property among his sons. Taking to the forest, he started to lead a life of solitude, absorbed in meditation.

Everything was well until one day, he happened to see a deer die, orphaning its just-born baby. Pitied by the sight, he decided to look after the fawn.

He bathed it, decorated it with garlands, fed it, and played with it. Even while sitting for meditation, he would open his eyes every now and then to see if the young deer was safe.

His attachment to the deer grew so strong that he barely ever had any time to practice meditation. Even at the time of death, all he could think about was the deer.

Thus, he was reborn in the form of a deer in the next life. However, due to the strength of his good deeds in the past, he had a recollection of his past life and felt ashamed of himself. Throughout his existence as the deer, he kept to the hermitage of sages, so that he would always remember the true purpose of life.

Thus, gradually, he abandoned the body of the deer and was born again as the son of a priest. He was born with a strong determination to realize the Soul in this birth, because of which he spent all his time in solitude.

Within no time, he realized the Soul, and became content.

*

"Thus," said Mrs. Nair. "I have told you the stories of all the three kings!"

"Thank you," said Narendra.

"Now, let us go back to the story of Nachiketas!"

Chapter Twelve

The main concern of Nachiketas was that even if he does practice meditation regularly, and does somehow succeed in realizing the Soul, what good will it do him when he dies.

It is necessary to remember that Nachiketas's understanding of the Soul is just theoretical at this point. He has not had direct realization of the Soul. Therefore, before he begins his endeavor, he wants confirmation from Lord Yama, who has personally realized the Soul, that the Soul is indeed eternal.

However, Lord Yama shook his head, and said, "Please ask for something else!"

When Nachiketas did not respond positively, Yama added, "Ask for long life! Ask for healthy sons and grandsons! Ask for cattle, elephants, horses and gold! Ask for a vast kingdom if you want, but do not ask me this!"

Chapter Thirteen

"When Lord Yama had no problem in talking about the process of meditation, through which the Soul can be realized, why is he so reluctant in discoursing directly on the Soul?" asked Narendra.

"Well," said Mrs. Nair, "This reluctance is not unique to Lord Yama. It can also be seen in all the great Masters of the past, whenever a student approaches them to know about the Soul!"

"Why?"

"They are all reluctant to talk about the Soul to everyone because the Soul is not an object, which can be grasped by the mind through the process of hearing about It from someone.

"All our knowledge is limited to the concepts of space and time. The Soul, which is beyond the concepts of space and time, cannot be expressed through any amount of words because they are all confined to the narrow experiences that we receive through the senses. All our explanations and descriptions are relative. That is, we can only say that an object is either similar or dissimilar to some other object.

"However, the Soul is not like anything known to us, and therefore, It cannot be clearly described using comparisons. The only way to know the Soul is to be It."

"Some vague understanding is better than ignorance, isn't it?" asked Narendra.

"Intellectual understanding about the Soul is as useless as total ignorance," said Mrs. Nair. "A sick person cannot regain his health by merely keeping the medicine in his pocket. He has to consume it, if he wants to be cured. In the same way, the Soul has to be attained if you want to know It."

"Then what is the use of these Masters, if they can't teach us about the Soul?"

"Even though the Soul cannot be taught directly, various clues pertaining to It can be imparted to those students who are detached from the objects of the senses, and have a well-controlled mind.

"These two qualifications – detachment from the objects of the senses and control over the mind – are inevitable in a student, who desires to learn about the Soul from a Master."

"Why is that?" asked Narendra.

"Since the beginning of our existence," said Mrs. Nair, "learning has been an external process, which involves the mind flowing through the senses towards their respective objects, and collecting new information. However, the knowledge of the Soul is an inward journey, which requires the senses, as well as the mind, to withdraw from their usual occupations and merge with the intellect.

"A casual curiosity on the part of the student will only help him to assimilate all the symbolic information on the Soul provided by the Master, and store them along with all the other data already existing in his mind. This new data, just like any other data that enters the mind, will clash with other contradictory information already existent therein, and create a chain reaction of sorts, which will lead to nothing but chaos and confusion.

"Such a student, in his attempt to understand the Soul, will not only fail in realizing It, but also lose whatever little peace of mind he had. His confused mind will make it extremely difficult for him to differentiate between the good and the bad; and chances are that he might make wrong choices in life, which will ultimately lead to his spiritual downfall.

"This state of utter confusion is beautifully described by Sage Vyasa through the condition of Arjuna, who was the grandfather of King Pareekshith, in the first chapter of the Bhagavad Gita. Fortunately, for Arjuna, he had Lord Krishna by his side, who uplifted him from this confusion through His divine discourse.

"However, most students are not so fortunate like Arjuna, and may end up destabilizing their mind in their attempt to reach the Soul. Even in the case of Arjuna, Lord Krishna did not help him immediately. The Lord waited until he calmed down completely and surrendered wholeheartedly, before narrating his famous discourse."

Chapter Fourteen

"Please tell me more about the Bhagavad Gita," said Narendra.

"The Bhagavad Gita is found in the Mahabharata and it consists of seven hundred verses," said Mrs. Nair. "It is the counsel of Lord Krishna to Arjuna in the middle of a battlefield!"

"Who were they fighting? And why?"

"When King Pandu died, the kingdom of Hastinapura was taken over by his blind brother, Dhritarashtra. However, when Yudhishtira, the eldest son of Pandu, became mature enough to rule the land, the blind king refused to leave his throne. Instead, he offered a small wasteland for the sons of Pandu.

"However, Yudhishtira and his brothers, popularly known as the Pandavas, built a magical kingdom in that wasteland. Possessed by envy, the sons of Dhritarashtra, popularly known as the Kauravas, tricked the Pandavas in a game of dice and forced them to leave the kingdom for thirteen years.

"When the stipulated period ended, the Kauravas refused to give them their land back. Lord Krishna Himself took the role of a messenger and tried to bargain for at least a smaller piece of land for the Pandavas. However, despite repeated attempts, the Kauravas refused to budge. Thus, having no other choice, the Pandavas declared war!

"This war was fought in the battlefield of Kurukshetra and it lasted for eighteen days! In the end, the Pandavas won!"

"When did Lord Krishna advice Arjuna?" Narendra asked.

"It was at that precise moment, when war was about to begin!" said Mrs. Nair. "However, the Mahabharata presents the Bhagavad Gita after ten days of war, through the words of Sanjaya, who repeats the counsel of Krishna to his master, Dhritarashtra!"

"I would like to understand the basic message of the Bhagavad Gita," said Narendra. "Could you please condense it for me?"

"Sure," said Mrs. Nair. "Pay attention!"

Chapter Fifteen

Dhritarashtra asked, "Assembled in the sacred land of Kurukshetra, with a desire to fight against each other, what did my sons and the sons of my deceased brother – Pandu, do, O Sanjaya?"

Sanjaya said, "O King, as the war was about to begin, Arjuna – the third son of Pandu, uttered the following words to his maternal cousin, Lord Krishna, who had assumed the role of his charioteer!

"O Krishna, place my chariot in the middle of both the armies," said Arjuna. "I want to observe all these warriors, who have arrayed here with a desire to fight, so that I may know who my opponents are in this war!"

Sanjaya said, "O King, having been addressed thus by Arjuna, Lord Krishna placed that excellent chariot, carried by fair horses, in the middle of both the armies! Arjuna saw stationed therein sires, grandsires, preceptors, uncles, brothers, sons, grandsons and friends! Seeing his relatives, Arjuna was overcome with extreme pity and dejection!"

Arjuna said, "O Krishna, herein, I see my own people assembled to fight! My limbs weaken, while my throat feels parched; also, my body shivers and is sprouting gooseflesh!

"O Krishna, I perceive conflicting omens, and am unable to see any good in killing my own people! Therefore, O Krishna, I desire neither victory, nor the pleasures of the kingdom! What use is this kingdom, or the pleasurable life that it has to offer?"

Sanjaya said, "Uttering these words, Arjuna sat down within his chariot in the middle of the battlefield, dropping his bow and arrows, deeply inflicted by sorrow! To him, who sat teary-eyed, overcome with pity and dejection, Krishna said these words!"

Lord Krishna said, "From where have this delusion entered you at this terrible hour, O Arjuna? It does not suit a warrior like you, and will certainly result in infamy!"

Arjuna said, "How can I attack the likes of my grandsire and preceptor, who deserve to be worshipped, with arrows in this war? I, who am in a helpless and confused state, ask You about what is right for me! Please explain to me, who am Your disciple, about that which is definitively great, for I take refuge in You!"

Sanjaya said, "Smiling, Lord Krishna uttered these words to the confused warrior, who had taken refuge in Him!"

Lord Krishna said, "You speak like a wise man, and yet grieve over that which is undeserving of grief; for, a wise man grieves neither over the departed, nor over the living!

"O Arjuna, death is certain for the born, and birth is certain for the dead! Just as the Soul attains childhood, youth and old-age in one body, in the same way, it attains another body; the wise are not deluded about it!

"These bodies are perishable, while the Soul is said to be eternal, imperishable and immeasurable; therefore, renouncing all grief, fight, O Arjuna!

"Just as a person abandons his old cloth to wear a new one, the Soul abandons an old body to accept a new one! The Soul in all bodies can never be slain, O Arjuna; therefore, there is no need for you to grieve over the fate of these warriors!

"However, if you do not fight this righteous war, then, having abandoned your natural course of action, you will incur sin! Treating alike pleasure and pain, gain and loss, victory and defeat, fight in this war, O Arjuna, and you will incur no sin!

"Your authority lies only in action, not in its results! Therefore, do not be concerned with the results of your actions; also, do not take to inaction! An individual cannot remain inactive even for a moment; everyone helplessly acts under the influence of their natural temperaments!

"You should perform actions based on your own nature, for action is greater than inaction! Without action, even the mere sustenance of the body is not possible!

"Therefore, always perform your actions with detachment, for by working in detachment, one can attain the Supreme! All actions are performed due to the qualities born of nature! However, deluded by the ego, a person considers himself the doer!

"Profitless actions according to one's own nature are better than beneficial actions against one's nature! If following one's nature will result in death, it is still better; actions against one's nature are riddled with fear!"

Arjuna said, "In that case, O Krishna, influenced by what does a person act against his nature, as if forced?"

Lord Krishna said, "It is under the influence of 'desires' that a person acts against his nature; it agitates the mind, causing confusion and doubt!

"Just as a mirror covered by dirt does not reflect anything clearly, in the same way, a mind covered by desires does not think clearly, O Arjuna!

Therefore, transcend all desires by directing your mind towards Me, for I am the abode of absolute contentment! I am the Ultimate Cause of everything!"

Arjuna said, "You stand before me in this finite form as my dear cousin and friend, and yet proclaim that You are the Ultimate Cause of everything that exists! If You really are the Supreme Lord, then why am I not able to perceive You in Your True Form?

Lord Krishna said, "You, as well as everyone else, have been bound within the delusory shell of individuality, and therefore perceive everything to be separate and different from you!

"However, in reality, there is no diversity, because I alone exist at all times! I am the Unborn, Immortal, Essence of everything! Actions do not bind Me, nor do I have any need for the fruits of actions!

"He, who truly understands my divine birth and actions, is not reborn on abandoning the body, for he attains Me, O Arjuna!

I am the origin, as well as the end of all things! There is nothing higher than Me, O Arjuna! All this exist in Me, like waves in the ocean! Those who take refuge in Me, transcend the delusory perception of diversity, which is the root cause of all suffering!

"Four kinds of people worship Me, O Arjuna – the sufferers, the curious, the wealth-seekers, and the wise! Among them, the wise alone excel, for they are solely devoted to Me! The wise worship Me undividedly because they want to transcend the cycle of births and deaths, and attain Me!"

Chapter Sixteen

Arjuna said, "O Lord, please describe to me the right process to attain You, so that I too can transcend this cycle of births and deaths!"

Lord Krishna said, "Whatever one contemplates throughout his life, he thinks of that alone at the time of death! Whatever one thinks of at the time of death, he attains that after leaving the body!

"Therefore, contemplate on Me at all times, and perform all your actions as an offering unto Me! I am easily attained by him, who remembers Me at all times, without thinking of anything else, O Arjuna! Having attained Me, he is not born again!

"I pervade this entire world invisibly; all beings exist in Me, I do not dwell in them!

"As the all-pervading air rests in space, in the same way, all beings exist in Me! Therefore, O Arjuna, you should worship Me at all times with a focused mind, knowing me as the Eternal Source of all beings!

"Those who worship Me undividedly at all times, I fulfill and secure all their needs! All beings are the same to Me; therefore, whoever worships Me wholeheartedly shall certainly attain Me, irrespective of their character!

"Even if the most sinful worship Me undividedly, they should be regarded as virtuous, for they soon become righteous and peaceful! O Arjuna, know that My devotees will never perish!

"Therefore, realizing Me as the source of everything, the wise worship Me with supreme devotion! With their mind absorbed in Me, always speaking of Me and enlightening one another, they revel! Dwelling within their hearts, I destroy the darkness of ignorance by lighting the lamp of knowledge!"

Arjuna said, "Even though I believe You, O Krishna, due to my ignorance, I am unable to contemplate on Your Form as the Supreme Lord! Therefore, please describe to me the Form in which I should meditate on You!"

Lord Krishna said, "O Arjuna, I am the Self, seated in the heart of all beings! I am the seed of all beings; nothing can exist without Me! Knowing the entire cosmos to be My body, O Arjuna, you should meditate on My Cosmic Form!"

Arjuna said, "O Great Lord! If You think it is possible for me to see It, then please reveal to me Your Cosmic Form!"

Lord Krishna said, "Your mortal eyes will not be able to behold My Cosmic Form; therefore, I give you a divine-eye to perceive It!"

Sanjaya said, "Having said this, Lord Krishna revealed His Cosmic Form before Arjuna! There, in the body of the God of gods, Arjuna saw the entire cosmos! Filled with wonder, Arjuna joined his palms and bowed his head!"

Arjuna said, "I see You everywhere, with endless arms, stomachs, mouths, and eyes; I see neither the beginning, nor the middle, nor the end of Your form, O Lord!

"On seeing Your Immeasurable Form, with fiery mouths, which are devouring all these great warriors, I am terrified, O Lord!

"Tell me who You are, O Supreme Lord, for I am unable to understand Your manifestation!"

Lord Krishna said, "I am Time, engaged in destroying everything! Even if you do not fight, these warriors here will not survive!

Therefore, arise and attain glory; destroy these enemies and cherish the kingdom! Be a mere instrumental cause for their death, O Arjuna, for they have already been slain by Me!"

Sanjaya said, "Having heard the thunderous words of Krishna, Arjuna prostrated before the Supreme Lord!"

Arjuna said, "Salutations to You, O Divine One! You are the Sole Refuge of the whole universe! I am unable to bear the sight of Your Great Form, O Lord! Therefore, have mercy on me, and please assume Your previous form as my beloved friend and cousin!"

Sanjaya said, "Thus requested, Lord Krishna again assumed His gentle form!"

Lord Krishna said, "It is indeed very difficult to see this Cosmic Form of Mine, which you have seen! O Arjuna, know that I can be realized in this Form only through undivided devotion!"

Arjuna said, "O Lord, should I worship You in this Form, or should I worship You as the Formless? Which is better?"

Lord Krishna said, "Even though both type of worship eventually leads to Me, it is better to worship Me in this Form, for it is difficult to contemplate on the Formless!

"Mentally renouncing all actions in Me, having Me as your Ultimate Goal, fix your mind in Me! By thus fixing your mind in Me, you shall overcome all obstacles through My grace!

"Offering all your actions unto Me, fight for My sake, and you shall incur no sin!

"Thus, a great secret has been revealed to you by Me! after contemplating on My words, do as you please!

"O Arjuna, this secret should never be conveyed to a person, who is devoid of devotion!

"Devoted to Me, he, who will convey this supreme secret to My devotees, will certainly attain Me!

"Has your delusion ceased on hearing this discourse, O Arjuna?"

Arjuna said, "My delusion has been completely destroyed, O Krishna! All my doubts have been dispelled, and I am ready to follow your counsel!"

Sanjaya said, "Blessed am I for having heard this wonderful dialogue between Lord Krishna and Arjuna! I salute the blessed Sage Vyasa, by whose grace I was able to gain this divine wisdom!

"O King, remembering this sacred dialogue between Lord Krishna and Arjuna, I am ecstatic!

"Wherever there is Krishna – the Supreme Lord, along with Arjuna – the resolute devotee, there will be prosperity, victory, joy, and certainty; this is my firm conviction!"

Chapter Seventeen

"This is the essence of the Bhagavad Gita! If you study this carefully, you will always be successful in life!" said Mrs. Nair.

"Even though I understand the truth in the words of Krishna, I am still not able to understand how Arjuna could muster the courage to fight," said Narendra. "Those were his relations in the opposite army. Even if he realizes the immortality of the Soul, wouldn't he still miss his relations when they are gone?"

"All our relationships are transient, dear child," said Mrs. Nair. "They exist only in the physical plane. Spiritually, who can be related to whom, for all are the same!"

"Are you saying that the relationships in this world will last only till death?" asked Narendra. "Once a person dies, then his Spirit is no longer concerned with us?"

"I will tell you the story of King Chitrakethu, listening to which, your doubt will be cleared," said Mrs. Nair.

"Ok," said Narendra.

Chapter Eighteen

Long ago, there was a king named Chitrakethu, who had many wives and yet no child to inherit the throne from him. Aggrieved by this, he approached Sage Angiraa and asked for his help.

Pitying the plight of the king, the sage performed a powerful Vedic ritual, as a result of which, the king obtained a son through his eldest wife.

Watching the king shower all his love towards the queen and her son, the other wives of the king became jealous. Realizing the newborn child to be the source of their misery, they poisoned him.

Hearing the news of his son's death, the king collapsed on the floor and started wailing like a child. As the ministers of the king stood watching helplessly, Sage Narada arrived, accompanied by Sage Angiraa.

"Cry not, O King," said Sage Angiraa, "for the will of fate is too strong to be changed!"

"How can you ask me to not cry, O Sage," asked Chitrakethu. "He was my only son! He was just a baby!"

"I think the only one who can console you now is the Spirit of your son," said Sage Narada.

The king stopped crying and gapingly watched the sage summon the Spirit of his dead son. Within moments, the Spirit arrived.

"O Spirit," said Sage Narada. "Please console your father, who is lamenting at your death!"

"Which father?" asked the Spirit. "I have taken countless births, O Sage, and in each birth, I have had a different father and mother."

"Don't you remember me, Son," asked Chitrakethu, springing to his feet.

"Your son is the body your wife gave birth to," said the Spirit. "I am not your son! I am no one's son! I am immortal, without beginning or end!"

The king was shocked to hear the reply. As he thus stood staring disbelievingly at the effulgent form, the Spirit vanished.

"It is pointless to weep for the death of the body, for it was always meant to die," said Sage Narada. "It is pointless to weep for the Soul, for it never dies! Abandon this petty emotion and realize the truth about death!"

*

"Thus enlightened by the sage," said Mrs. Nair, "Chitrakethu renounced his grief and became peaceful!"

"Thank you for telling me this story," said Narendra.

"You are welcome," said Mrs. Nair. "Now, shall we proceed to the story of Nachiketas?"

"Yes," said Narendra.

Chapter Nineteen

Lord Yama does not want to push the young mind of Nachiketas in to that dark ditch of confusion, which Arjuna had fallen in, by handing him such a dangerous knowledge without evaluating his capacity. Therefore, he wants to first test the detachment of the student, and tempts him with all the material pleasures that his young mind can imagine.

However, Nachiketas is not an ordinary student. After all, he had willfully arrived at the abode of Yama just to fulfill the wish of his father. Even the fact that he had the presence of mind to ask regarding the Soul to the God of Death is itself a proof of the fact that Nachiketas was a brilliant boy.

Smiling at the tempting offer made by Lord Yama, Nachiketas said, "By offering me all the fortunes of the mortal world, you have proven beyond doubt that the boon I ask for is far superior to them! Therefore, I do not want anything else! Please just answer my question!"

"I will arrange for the pleasures of the heaven for you in this very world," said Lord Yama. "I will give you an unending supply of heavenly delicacies! I will make the celestial beauties dance and sing for you! I will keep your body youthful! O Nachiketas, take any of these, but do not ask me about the Soul!"

As calm as ever, Nachiketas said, "Ephemeral are these things that you have offered to me, O God of Death! They will only result in the dissipation of my energy! Therefore, keep the dance and song to yourself, and tell me about the Soul!"

Lord Yama's eyes brightened and he smiled, for nothing could be more pleasing to a Master than a worthy student. Placing his right palm over the head of the boy as a sign of blessing, Lord Yama said, "May you live a long, healthy life, O Nachiketas, for I am extremely pleased with you!"

After a brief pause, Lord Yama continued, "There are two paths in this world – the pleasant and the good! Fools choose the pleasant, while the wise choose the good! You are wise, O Nachiketas, for you have chosen the good path!"

Chapter Twenty

"Could you please explain the difference between the two paths?" asked Narendra.

"Of course," said his mother. "An individual can choose to either revel in the momentary pleasures of the senses, which are easily obtained, or strive to experience the eternal contentment of the Soul, which is difficult to attain. Sensual pleasures are enjoyable at first, but will ultimately result in death, while realization of the Soul offers eternal contentment, and results in immortality. Therefore, the path of the senses is called 'the pleasant', while the path of the Soul is called 'the good'."

"I see," said Narendra.

"These two paths are beautifully suggested in the Mahabharata, when both Arjuna and Duryodhana (eldest son of Dhritarashtra) arrive at Dwaraka, the palace of Lord Krishna, to ask for his support in the war."

"Please tell me that story!" said Narendra.

"Ok," said Mrs. Nair.

Chapter Twenty One

Lord Krishna was sleeping when the princes reached His palace at Dwaraka. Therefore, they decided to patiently wait for Him to wake up. Duryodhana, who had arrived first, sat on a throne near the head of Krishna, while Arjuna sat on the floor at the feet of the Lord.

When Lord Krishna opened his eyes, he saw Arjuna first and greeted him.

"I am here too," screamed Duryodhana, springing to his feet.

"How are you, Duryodhana?" asked Krishna. "I hope all is well at Hastinapura!"

"Yes, yes," said Duryodhana. "Everything is good there. I just came here to ask for your support in the war!"

"I too have come for that same purpose, my Lord," said Arjuna.

"Ah, yes, the war," said Krishna. "Well, you both are equal to me, so I will have to support you both! However, since I can't be on both sides simultaneously, I am willing to offer my huge army to one side, while staying unarmed with the other side!"

Duryodhana opened his mouth to claim the army, but was stopped by Krishna.

"I saw Arjuna first," said the Lord, "therefore, the choice is his!"

Duryodhana growled at first, then, reluctantly agreed.

"I choose You," said Arjuna.

"What a fool!" thought Duryodhana, suppressing a smile.

"Remember," said Lord Krishna, "I will not fight! No matter what, I will not pick up arms! Is that alright to you?"

"Yes, my Lord," said Arjuna. "Your mere presence is sufficient for me! If it pleases You, then please be my charioteer and guide me to victory!"

"So be it," said Krishna.

The joy of Duryodhana knew no bounds. He was certain that Arjuna had made the wrong choice. However, had Arjuna chosen otherwise, then he would have never obtained the timely counsel of Lord Krishna before the war, when he had completely lost his morale. Most probably, he would have abandoned the war, and the Pandavas would have lost.

*

"However," said Mrs. Nair, "Arjuna chose the good path instead of the

pleasant!”
     “I see,” said Narendra.
     “Now let us proceed to the story of Nachiketas!”
     “Ok!”

Chapter Twenty Two

After thus praising the determination of Nachiketas and glorifying the path of the Soul, Lord Yama said, "The Soul is never born, nor does It ever die! It is unborn, eternal, and ancient! It is not slain, even when the body is slain!

"It is smaller than the smallest, and greater than the greatest! It is seated in the heart of all beings! Only he, who has no desires and is free from grief, can see the greatness of the Soul! It is not attained through discourses! It cannot be grasped by the intellect! It is attained by him, who chooses It alone! To him, this Soul reveals Its own nature! He, who is neither peaceful, nor focused, can never attain the knowledge of this Soul, O Nachiketas!"

After having attentively heard all the hints on the nature of the Soul provided by Lord Yama, Nachiketas asked, "What is the relation of the Soul to the body? Please explain this to me!"

Nodding, Lord Yama said, "Know that the body is like a chariot, and the Soul is the Lord of this chariot! The intellect is the charioteer, and the mind is the rein! The senses are the horses, and their objects are the roads! He, whose mind is firmly held by the intellect, completes the journey of life by attaining the supreme state!

"The true purpose of this vehicle is not to undertake an external excursion of the senses towards their respective objects. It is to achieve an inward transcendence towards the ultimate essence!"

"Please explain this transcendence in detail," said Nachiketas.

Lord Yama replied, "Beyond the senses are their experiences, beyond the experiences is the mind, beyond the mind is the intellect, and beyond the intellect is the Soul! Beyond the Soul is the Invisible, beyond the Invisible is God! Beyond God, there is nothing! He is the ultimate!"

Chapter Twenty Three

"Yama began his discourse by referring to It as the Soul, and continued to do so until this very point," said Narendra. "Now, he offers two new words – the Invisible and God. Why?"

"It is called the Soul only with respect to an individual," said Mrs. Nair. "When this individuality is transcended, It becomes the Invisible Essence pervading the entire cosmos. When even the cosmos is transcended, It becomes God.

"When condensing the Bhagavad Gita, I had mentioned a sentence, which is the fourth verse of the ninth chapter of the original Bhagavad Gita, where Lord Krishna says, 'This entire cosmos is pervaded by Me in My invisible form; all beings exist in Me, I do not dwell in them!'

"Lord Krishna is herein expressing two states. With respect to the cosmos, He is the Invisible Essence, which pervades everything. However, in His essential nature, He is God, beyond the cosmos."

"I do not understand!" said Narendra.

"God is everywhere," said Mrs. Nair. "He is in the mountains, He is in the rivers, He is in the ocean! However, He is neither the mountain, nor the river, nor the ocean. He is the essence of all these things. Therefore, with respect to the world, He is invisible!

"Now, when the world in entirely transcended, then there is nothing left but Him. Therefore, even the word 'invisible' becomes insufficient to describe Him. Hence, He is called God!"

"I see," said Narendra.

"Let us go back to Yama's discourse," said Mrs. Nair.

Chapter Twenty Four

Yama continued, "A wise man should dissolve his senses in the mind, the mind in the intellect, the intellect in the Soul, and the Soul in God! The wise say that this path is difficult to tread because it is as sharp as the edge of a razor!"

*

"Hey, I have heard the phrase 'razor's edge path' before," said Narendra.

"Yes," said Mrs. Nair. "This is one of the most famous declarations of Lord Yama, and it is a strong warning to all the students of spirituality.

"Reading about the process of transcendence mentioned by Lord Yama, and then imagining about it, might give rise to a delusory sense of confidence in the student that this task is very easy to achieve. Such a false confidence will make the student careless, and thereby result in his downfall.

"Therefore, the God of Death warns us all that the path towards God is as sharp as the edge of a razor, wherein one must tread with the utmost care and vigilance."

"I will be careful," said Narendra.

"Good," said his mother.

Chapter Twenty Five

With a sigh, Lord Yama concluded, "He – who realizes that, which is soundless, formless, changeless, tasteless, odorless, without either a beginning or an end – is liberated from death!"

*

Mrs. Nair continued, "Nachiketas felt elated at the answer he had received. His question was simple, 'What happens after death? Do I end? Or do I continue?'

"Through his discourse, Lord Yama explained to him that death was not the end. It is the body that is born and it is the body that dies. The Soul is immortal. It existed even before the body was born. It will continue to exist even when the body dies."

"I see," said Narendra.

"Remember what Lord Krishna said in the Bhagavad Gita, 'Just as a person discards his old clothes to wear new ones, the Soul discards an old body to wear a new one'," said Mrs. Nair

After a brief pause, she continued, "Thus, Lord Yama had fulfilled all the three boons he had promised to his young guest. Having received the permission and blessings of the God of Death, Nachiketas then returned to his home."

"What happened then?" asked Narendra.

"Just as Lord Yama had promised, Vajashravasa happily accepted his son, who had returned from the abode of death," said Mrs. Nair. "Spreading the wisdom he had received from his Master amongst rightful students, Nachiketas lived a long and prosperous life. To this day, his unusual story is remembered by all eager students of spirituality.

"It is believed that any person, who hears and retells this story of Nachiketas and Lord Yama, will have a successful life and thereby attain great glory."

"Thank you for telling me this wonderful story," said Narendra. "I feel a lot better now!"

"Good," said Mrs. Nair. "Remember, death is not the end!"

"I will," said Narendra, and hugged his mother.

www.ingramcontent.com/pod-product-compliance
Lightning Source LLC
Chambersburg PA
CBHW020944160726